Grief-Stricken
My Emotional Journey

A Devotion of Truth and Hope

Michelle D. Alexander

Shaneice,
Be encouraged, God Has You.

love [signature]

6-30-19

BookLocker

Published by BookLocker.com, Inc., St. Petersburg, Florida.

Printed on acid-free paper.

BookLocker.com, Inc.
2019

First Edition

Definitions from Merriam-Webster

Scriptures quoted from King James Version

Introduction

This is a chronicle of my journey with grief. I wrote this devotional to help me process the emotional highs and lows after my father's death. I chose the title "Grief-Stricken" because it explains the magnitude of my pain. Losing my father, Dr. H.A. Alexander, Sr., is by far the most difficult experience I've ever had. I soon realized the grief was too great to hold in and internalize, so I began to put my feelings on paper. Grief has no respect of religion or status. Being a Christian doesn't exempt anyone from this inevitable devastation. I hope in the process of sorting my misery, I can comfort others who are trying to sort their own.

I believe you are holding this book because you have suffered a loss. Before you turn this page, let me assure you that there is no time frame assigned to grief. As Christians, we need to know that losing a loved one is agonizing. Being a believer does not erase our emotions. We are human, and it is okay for us to hurt. I encourage you to give yourself permission to feel and to process every emotion that arises. The good, the bad, and the ugly, and believe me, it gets ugly. Don't be too hard on yourself when you can't deal with the flood of emotions. Though I have an amazing support system, there were times I was so filled with anger and rage that I didn't want to hear any words of encouragement. I didn't want the clichés that were supposed to comfort me. I wanted Daddy.

My father was an incredible man. He was full of love, wisdom, and faith. In fact, he was a superhero. My Superhero. Losing him sent me on an excruciating course, yet a necessary one. I had to learn how to keep living. Most days, I didn't even want to feel, but to stop feeling would mean to stop functioning. Even in my worst pain, I knew I had to keep living. The awesome legacy my father left, required me to live on.

No two journeys are the same because relationships are different, but all are filled with highs and lows. I know it may seem like you are, but no, you are not losing your mind. This ebb and flow is perfectly natural. One moment you think you can make it, then the next moment, you can't even breathe. A dark cloud of despair can rob a glimmer of hope.

When we are hurting, sometimes we don't even want to talk about the death we've seen. At other times, all we can talk about is death. The road to healing is complicated, uncertain, and extremely frustrating, but you can survive! You've picked up this book hoping to see the light in this situation. The light comes when we realize that though we've lost them, we don't have to lose who they *are* to us. They are still an important part of our lives.

While it's difficult to accept that I will never create new memories, I cherish my existing memories as precious jewels. Yet I understand that these memories are much more valuable. Memories of my father are irreplaceable. Honestly, even the happy recollections can be painful. I'm living in a new normal that doesn't feel normal at all. Nevertheless, it's my reality. I often feel as though my healing was and still is, short-lived. As I take my time through my emotions, I realize this is just part of the process. There will always be good days and bad days. There is no reason to be ashamed. In fact, it is a testament to the depth of my love for my father. His profound impact on me warrants that I remember him in the way he loved me! I'm not encouraging you to stay in a place of grief or turmoil, but to allow yourself to feel every emotion that comes with saying goodbye.

I have gained great compassion for others on their journey. It's important for believers to have compassion for one another. We should not judge others who are on this very painful and uncertain passage. It adds more anguish to an already painful situation. For example, when I missed "special" church functions, there were church people who felt it necessary to judge me. It wasn't just done in private, but to my face. They questioned the commitment of my relationship with God. One person asked me if I had left God? That is a ridiculous question! God is the only reason I'm still standing. To cope with my grief, I had to take time away for myself. When people are looking at you with pity in their eyes, it can make you shy away. When people are shaming you for still grieving, it makes you feel as if your salvation is on trial. The truth is they may not know how to express sympathy, but some people care. Sadly, there are those who wish you would just get over it already. They want you to move on. They tell you to be strong, but they want you to pretend you're not hurting. If you deal with those people, I want you to know you don't need anyone's permission to grieve. Be where you are. I won't judge you. I understand the journey all too well.

I'm praying for you as you turn every page. Know that God isn't punishing you. He wants to heal your heart. Healing will begin when you are open to your emotions and give God permission to hold your hand.

He giveth power to the faint; and to them that have no might he increaseth strength. Isaiah 40:29

YOU LEFT WITHOUT MY PERMISSION

I wasn't ready to say goodbye.

I often ask the question, Lord, Why?

You left without my permission, you knew I wouldn't let you go.

I have so many questions and many more things I need to know.

A little more time is what I often wish for,

But God saw fit to call you home, so you wouldn't have to suffer anymore.

I'll cherish your last words to me. "I love you, sweetheart."

Nothing can rob me of that moment, not even us being apart.

I'll hold on tight to every moment that we had,

I'll love you for the rest of my days, MY PROTECTOR, MY HERO, MY DAD!

Confused: (of a person) unable to think clearly; bewildered.

I couldn't understand what was happening. Dad was doing okay just seven hours ago. As I got ready to leave the hospital just seven short hours ago, I had no idea, "I love you, sweetheart", would be the last words I would ever hear him say. Bittersweet. Those are the sweetest words ever spoken, and I'd never hear him say them again. My emotions are deeper than just words. I know for a fact that my daddy loved me, and I love him. I knew my dad's love for me was without limitation. He would've given me the world. Well actually, he did. To me, he was my world! He gave me so much, taught me so much, and instilled so much wisdom in me.

My transparent moment: I don't understand what just happened. How did this happen? Why so suddenly? Why now? How do I keep going without one of the greatest influences in my life? I'm dumbfounded. What's next? As I try to make sense of what has happened and try to process this flood of emotions, I look to God. Lord help me understand the journey…

Let my cry come near before thee, O Lord: give me understanding according to thy word. Psalms 119:169

A Prayer For Today: Lord when I'm confused and lack understanding, help me to understand your word and your perfect plan for my life. Amen.

Broken Hearted: overcome by grief or despair

The most painful thing I've ever had to experience. My heart literally shattered as I stood in the Intensive Care Unit waiting room at the Veterans Affairs Hospital talking to the head surgeon. Her words to our family were, "Have you all ever discussed with your dad what measures should be taken to preserve his life?" As I felt what was coming next, my lips began to quiver. Instinctively, I responded to her question in the only way possible for me. "He would want everything to be done to save his life". The doctor looked at me with despair in her eyes and said, "We are JUST ABOUT AT EVERYTHING". The strength in my legs wanted to leave me, but somehow, I stayed upright. It felt like, within minutes, the announcement came overhead "Code Blue".

Tears run hot as I cry and pray to God to not let it be true. Not my daddy. It is true. Dad is GONE! Attempting to make my way to his

ICU room, the strength in my legs left me. I lay in the hospital hallway screaming at the top of my lungs. My hero, my dad, my protector, my everything is GONE! I feel as though my heart is being ripped clean from my body. Shattering like glass.

My transparent moment: Grief-stricken, I can't breathe. Lord, how am I supposed to go on from here?

The Lord is nigh unto them that are of a broken heart; and saveth such as be of a contrite spirit. Psalms 34:18

The journey begins…

> *Prayer For Today: Lord you know what I need, my world is shattered, and my heart is broken. Wrap your loving arms around me, I need your comfort and strength more than ever. Please be with me during this difficult journey. Amen.*

Shock: a sudden or violent mental or emotional disturbance

This is sudden and unexpected. Just a few hours ago, my dad was telling me he loved me.

September 14, 2017. I hear the doctor declare: "time of death 4:22 a.m.". I am in total and complete shock. Again, my legs can't hold me, and I collapse to the floor. My world has been completely shattered. I can't bring myself to believe this is really happening. When I finally get up, I still cannot accept what I heard. As I'm looking at Daddy lying in that hospital bed, lifeless, I beg him to get up. "Daddy please, wake up." I plead with him for several minutes to please get up, hoping the doctor made a mistake. When I don't get the response I want, it feels like a huge boulder slams into my chest and I can't breathe. This is the worst day of my life. I see my family's reaction to this devastating news, and it crushes me even more. Somebody, anybody, please tell me this is not real. Please tell me my Daddy is not gone.

My transparent moment: As my emotions spin out of control, I realize that I'm not speaking. I can't even verbalize what I'm feeling. Standing here, my body shakes and my heart stops. This is surreal. Everything seems to move in slow motion. Why Lord, why? The only thing I'm sure of is that we need the Lord to help and give us comfort. We can't do this alone.

Blessed are they that mourn: for they shall be comforted. Matthew 5:4

The journey continues...

> *Prayer For Today: Lord, I am at a loss for words. The tears won't stop flowing, but I know you're able to comfort me. Do it for me Lord! Amen.*

Grief-stricken: overcome with deep sorrow.

On September 14, 2017, my life changed. I experienced a sorrow I've never felt. The loss massive and the impact gut-wrenching. Words cannot adequately describe the depth of my pain.

I have zero control over my emotions. At this moment, I am not capable of holding it together. I don't even know what to do next. I wait for someone to tell me there's been a mistake, and my dad is not gone. That doesn't happen. My world, as I know it, has been flipped completely upside down.

In the most unthinkable agony, I sit and wonder if it will ever end? There seems to be a never-ending well of tears. I cry until I don't even have the strength to lift my head.

My transparent moment: I hope that God can hear my heart's prayer through its shattered pieces. I wouldn't wish this pain on anyone. Words escape me, and all I can think is Lord, you know.

And God shall wipe away all tears from their eyes; and there shall be no more death, neither sorrow, nor crying, neither shall there be any more pain: for the former things are passed away. Revelation 21:4

The journey continues...

Prayer For Today: Lord, you KNOW! Amen.

Helpless: lacking protection or support; unable to do something to make a situation, task, etc., better or easier

What do I do now? Despite my education, background, and relationship with God, there is nothing I can personally do to make this situation better. My go-to person is gone.

Daddy was MY EVERYTHING! Protector, supporter, mentor, and provider, all gone in the blink of an eye. I know that death is a part of life, but you can never be prepared for it. It hits you like a ton of bricks and breaks you from the inside. I found myself feeling helpless. What do I do now? Who do I call? Where do I turn? So many questions, but no real answers or solutions in my very limited view.

In every situation, I reached out to my dad. To me, his absence is the same as saying I have no one left. I feel like I'm five years old again, and I just want Daddy. He'll know what to do. Try telling this 5-year-old that her daddy can't fix any and everything, Impossible.

Before September 14, 2017, there was never a day I had to live without my daddy, I can barely breathe realizing this is my reality every day from here on out. Sure, I know he's in my heart, but I want him here; plain and simple!

My transparent moment: Truth is, I can't see past my pain. If help was staring me in the face, I wouldn't know it. As I search for answers and help, I enlist the help of my heavenly Father. I close my eyes and I can hear my mom singing the old familiar hymn by Charles Wesley, "Father, I stretch my hands to thee. No other help I know".

I will lift up mine eyes unto the hills, from whence cometh my help.

My help cometh from the LORD, which made heaven and earth. Psalms 121:1-2

This painful journey continues...

> *Prayer For Today: Lord I stretch out my hands to you.*
> *Please help me in my time of need. Amen.*

Dread: to feel extreme reluctance to meet or face.

I don't look forward to the hard days ahead: planning Daddy's funeral, the services to celebrate his life, the finality of his burial. Just the thought is more than I can bear. Reality begins to set in. Life without Daddy was something I never imagined. There will be no more of his jokes or encouraging words. No more rescuing me. I'll miss him preaching the walls down, and the big smile on his face while I'm up preaching. No more hearing him say "Put your weight on it!" when I'm preaching. I can't face never seeing him in the congregation cheering on his baby girl. I don't want to face these dreadful moments, days, months, and years.

I'm ready to give up, but something on the inside won't let me. I won't let my daddy down by giving up. He always said, "Keep your head up, and stay prayerful". Daddy instilled the word of God in me and taught me to trust in God despite what I may be facing. *This* does not feel good, nor am I ready for the journey, but I'll push with the small morsel of push I have in me.

My transparent moment: I just don't want to do this. I want my daddy back. I know it doesn't work like that, but it's what I want!

"Be not dismayed whate'er betide, God will take care of you; Beneath His wings of love abide, God will take care of you."

Civilla D. Martin

Take therefore no thought for the morrow: for the morrow shall take thought for the things of itself. Sufficient unto the day is the evil thereof. Matthew 6:34

The journey continues...

Prayer For Today: Lord, I know that despite every situation and circumstance I face, you will be with me. I know that even when it doesn't feel good to me, you will take care of me and see me through. Be my light in these very dark and dreary days of my life. Amen.

Frustrated: feeling or expressing distress and annoyance, especially because of inability to change or achieve something.

As my nephew and I sit at the funeral home making the arrangements, I can't help being frustrated and wishing things were different. There is nothing within my power that I could've done to change the outcome. Dad is gone. God called him home, and now we are left here to pick up the pieces.

It's frustrating having to handle the business of deciding arrangements, dealing with insurance, and trying to figure out the best way to honor Dad and his legacy. My nephew and I have a huge job to do, and everyone is depending on us. What if we fail? How do we make this a celebration of life, a mandate to carry on the legacy, and a message of hope to our grieving family? How do we stand tall when the desire to stand is gone? When do *we* grieve? Are we allowed?

My nephew and I never spoke those words to each other, nor did we place any unrealistic expectations on one another. Instead, we held each other up. With confidence only God could provide, we stepped up to the task. There was no vote, no charge, just a task that fell on us. There was no conversation as to who would handle the arrangements. It was unspoken unanimously, we knew what we had to do. We were the two he had mentored, taught the word of God, and prepared for ministry. The two people he had entrusted with his pride and joy; "The Church". What an awesome opportunity to honor Dad, tell his story, and carry on his memory. Lord, please give us all the things we don't possess to be able to carry out this task and honor the greatest man we knew. What a journey! I wouldn't have chosen it, but I'm honored God has the confidence in us to walk this path together.

My transparent moment: When do I grieve? Why doesn't anyone ask if I can do this or if I'm okay?

Let not your heart be troubled: ye believe in God, believe also in me. John 14:1

The journey continues...

Prayer For Today: Lord help us the honor the Late Dr H.A. Alexander Sr. in the greatest way possible. Help us to show the love he gave, the love we feel, and the love that will forever live in our hearts. You have given us the awesome opportunity to share his story. Give us the strength we need to carry out this task. Emotions will run high at times, but you'll hold us up in our weakest moments. Amen.

Overwhelming: used to describe something that is so confusing, and difficult, that you feel unable to do it

Somehow overwhelmed does not fully explain how I'm feeling. I'm dealing with Dad's death, planning a Homegoing Celebration, taking care of family, taking care of church business, and the list continues. My mind is racing, and my heart is all over the place. I'm on the verge of a breakdown. This is all just too much. It's too much to feel. Too much to do. Too much to accept. I want to run away, but I quickly cancel that thought because my mom needs me. And I'm undoubtedly aware that running away won't take my pain away.

As painful as this is, I must allow myself to feel and go through this grieving process. I don't want to hold my emotions in. I'm learning that facing my feelings can be therapeutic. Despite the chaos going on in my mind and heart, I'll pause and whisper a prayer.

My transparent moment: My emotions are weighing heavily on my heart. I'm not sure I can do this.

Hear my cry, O God; attend unto my prayer. From the end of the earth will I cry unto thee, when my heart is overwhelmed: lead me to the rock that is higher than I. Psalms 61:1-2

And so, the journey continues...

Prayer For Today: Lord calm my mind and heart and help me with each task and obligation I have before me. Amen.

Numb: deprive of feeling or responsiveness.

As people flood my house, they share hugs, love, and words of condolences, I feel like I'm in the twilight zone. I've hugged so many people I've lost track. Now it has become a formality. My pain is so deep that the hugs and words can't even brush the surface of what I'm feeling. I know some people genuinely care, I just can't respond. I sit here knowing the deep pain in my eyes says everything my mouth and body cannot. I've cried to the point of exhaustion. I can't sleep or eat, but I know I must. So many of my family members are depending on me. I now must be *all* things to everyone, but how? That was Dad, not me. How do I pick up the pieces of my heart and hold the family together? I hear Dad's voice whisper "Keep your head up and stay prayerful". This was something Daddy always told us when we felt overwhelmed. Those words of encouragement resonate in my spirit and the numbness turns into comfort.

I can hear my dad remind us to remember the word of God tells us he will never leave us nor forsake us. Dad let us know everything we needed was in the word of God, and he was with us always. I remember when times were rough, Dad would say, "We're going to get through this with the help of God". I smile and thank God for this gentle reminder. I have a long journey ahead of me, but I thank God for allowing me to feel comforted during my great discomfort. I admonish myself I'm not leaning unto my own understanding. I've made it one more day. I have another chance to be everything my dad instilled in me and be who God has called me to be.

My transparent moment: I know people mean well, but they just can't penetrate my hurt. I'm numb.

Come unto me, all ye that labour and are heavy laden, and I will give you rest. Take my yoke upon you, and learn of me; for I am meek and lowly in heart: and ye shall find rest unto your souls. For my yoke is easy, and my burden is light. Matthew 11:28-30

The journey continues...

Prayer For Today: Lord, please help me. I just can't make it without your help. Hold me tight and please don't let me go. Amen.

Alone: separated from others: isolated

As I sit in a house full of people coming in and out, I feel so alone. I feel like a little girl waiting by the door for Daddy to come home from work. I convince myself that he's coming home; he's just running late. I stare at the door wishing Daddy would walk through and embrace me. When Daddy never comes, I silently beg to awake from this horrible nightmare. Despite the many people in the room, it feels like no one can hear my plea for help. I feel my heart bleeding out all over the floor, yet no one comes to my aid. It's like being thirsty and wanting someone to give me water, but I can't ask. I can't speak. I'm exhausted and dehydrated, but no one sees my need. Does anyone truly know the pain I'm feeling? Why aren't they helping me? The reality is no one can take away this pain. No one can fill this void in my life. My heart longs for one more conversation with my daddy, one more smile, one more hug, one more day. Now I understand what it means to be alone in a crowded room.

I zone in and out. I can barely follow any of the conversations in the room. A sense of abandonment has taken over. Why did Daddy have to leave me? A big part of me is now gone, and it's so unfair. I've been robbed. My stability has been pulled right from under me and my foundation shattered. I'm wandering around in a desolate and remote place; isolated from reality, everything, and everyone, and I beg God to help me. Where are you, God? I know you're near so please draw near to me. Daddy told me despite what's going on, God is standing by. I'm thankful for that. Although I feel alone, I am not alone. God and my family are with me. I also have amazing friends by my side every step of the way. Now, I have my own guardian angel watching over me, my daddy. Forever in my heart until we meet again.

My transparent moment: I know it sounds selfish, but I want my daddy back. I'm alone.

I will never leave thee nor forsake thee. Hebrews 13:5

The journey continues...

Prayer For Today: God I feel so alone, I know you promised never to leave me nor forsake me. Please draw near to me and shower me with your unwavering love. Amen.

Worried: mentally troubled or concerned: feeling or showing concern or anxiety about what is happening or might happen

As worry sets in, my mind works overtime trying to process what has happened and what's coming. I'm worried about my mom and her health. Will Dad's death cause her health to fail? I'm worried about my entire family. I have so many questions. How will we function without Daddy? I'm worried about the church family, too. Even though Daddy retired, Bethesda has never been without Dr. H.A. Alexander, Sr. What does the future hold? How do we cope? How do we make sense of it all? I can't stop my mind from racing. What now? What am I supposed to do? Daddy said this day would come, but am I prepared for what comes next? Like a television that gets louder at night when commercials come on, I want to silence the chaotic concern that is going through my mind. Even in the rare moments when I'm able to drop off to sleep and catch a nap, my mind still races with concerns of the unknown.

I close my eyes, take a deep breath, and pray for peace in my mind. I don't have answers, but the God I serve is the answer to every problem. I even worry if I'm even equipped for this journey.

My transparent moment: I have no clue of what to do, how to do it, or even why at this point in my life I must do it! I worry if I'm even equipped for this journey.

Casting all your care upon him; for he careth for you. 1 Peter 5:7

The journey continues...

> *Prayer For Today: Lord, my mind is all over the place and worry has set in. Give me peace and clarity. Please help me to maintain. Amen.*

Doubt: feel uncertain about.

I've been completely shaken to my core and the dark cloud of doubt hangs over me. I've questioned everything, I've even asked myself if my faith is strong enough to sustain me. I doubt my ability to endure, my ability to think rationally, and my ability to trust that I will get through this. At this moment I'm unable to see the silver lining or the sunshine. Ever since that dreaded Thursday, my days have been dark. My pain is so deep that my mind has not been able to grasp what I'm supposed to do now. I'm familiar with the cliché, "it gets better", but today, "better" is not within my reach. I'm reminded of something my Dad always told me, "Trust God always, even when you can't see it or don't understand it". In my quiet time, the Lord speaks and reminds me that his ways are not my ways, his thoughts are not my thoughts, and he is working on my behalf. While I don't understand everything, I've made my daily declaration: "Leaning not to my own understanding". It has been keeping me going.

I'm led to seek grief counseling. I realize that although I'm a Christian, and I seek his word daily, it is perfectly normal to get counseling. It might be good to talk my feelings out with someone who isn't affected by my dad's death. I don't have to be embarrassed about reaching out for help. I found someone not too far from my neighborhood. I realize after my first session that God was even in that process. I found a wonderful Christian grief counselor. She helped me talk through my emotions and confirmed what I've been feeling. It *is* okay to grieve and feel whatever you feel! Grief has many stages and going through them does not mean you are not trusting in God. I've found that even in these uncertain dark days, my relationship with God has become stronger, and my prayer every day is, "Lord, keep my mind".

My transparent moment: Life without Daddy seems so uncertain. I'm afraid I can't do this.

Trust in the LORD with all thine heart; and lean not unto thine own understanding. In all thy ways acknowledge him, and he shall direct thy paths. Proverbs 3:5-6

The journey continues...

Prayer For Today: Lord I ask you for guidance, reassurance, and peace because even full of doubt, there is still something in me that knows YOU will never lead me wrong. Amen.

Weak: lacking strength; mentally or intellectually deficient

During these very difficult days, I've felt weaker than I ever have. My body, mind, and spirit are drained. I have not been getting enough sleep and my appetite has not been the best. If only I could stop the constant racing in my mind. I feel a real sense of defeat. I wonder to myself if I have the strength to endure this pain. Physically, I lack the energy to endure on most days while longing for peace of mind.

Even the strongest people get weak and discouraged. I'm usually the one the family looks to for strength, but Dad's death has knocked the wind out of me and robbed me of my strength. During this extremely tough journey, I have given myself permission to feel how I feel. I don't have to be strong. I will have weak days, and it's okay. I remind myself that God did not promise sunshine without rain, heartache without pain, or joy without sorrow. I am a Christian and moments of weakness and despair does not determine the strength of my relationship with God. Despite how I feel, I still trust and believe God will get me through this. I have the blessed assurance that Jesus is mine, and when I am weak, he is strong.

My transparent moment: I don't want anyone to tell me that I must be strong.

And he said unto me, My grace is sufficient for thee: for my strength is made perfect in weakness. Most gladly therefore will I rather glory in my infirmities, that the power of Christ may rest upon me. 2 Corinthians 12:9

The journey continues...

Prayer For Today: Lord, although I am weak in this moment, strengthen me for the journey. Amen.

Depressed: a state of feeling sad: dejection ·anger, anxiety, and depression. low in spirits; downcast; despondent: Little or no desire to do anything.

As I lie in this bed, I have no desire to do anything. I can't find even a fiber of motivation. Depression has set in so heavy I wish I could just sleep the pain away. I don't want to go, do, or be. I wish I was invisible. I'm tired of people looking at me with pity in their eyes. I'm tired of people, by way of a word or gesture, encouraging me to just get over it already! And please stop saying that my dad would want me to be strong. I have to ask. Do they know my Dad well enough to tell me what he would want? Do they have insight into our lives that I am unaware of? Or are these people just trying to annoy me? At this point, I can't tell. Therefore, I need to stay in the house and cut off interaction with everyone. I've had enough. Now I'm at my "I will snap on you" mode. I'm so irritable and on edge, I just want to steer clear of people.

When the doorbell rings, I lie in this bed and ignore it until they leave. I'm not in control of my emotions. I've bottomed out, and I don't want to go a step further. Yes, I know, Mom needs me, my son needs me; everyone needs me. Unfortunately, I have no more to give, and I have resolved in my mind to throw in the towel.

I recall a conversation I had with my dad. He said, "There will come a day when I won't be here. You'll have to carry on and stand tall with your head up. The others will be depending on you". Daddy always told me I was smart and capable, and that I could handle anything with the help of God. It was just like him to let me know this right there amid "my pity party".

My dad was so proud of me; I dare not let him down. My rock, my hero is not here to cheer me on. I feel a moment of peace when I think of my Dad and how he could always say the right thing to make me smile. I muster up a little strength and hold my head up best I can. It's difficult, but I give it all I have. I'll make more progress tomorrow.

My transparent moment: How do I go on? How am I supposed to hold my head up or stand tall when I have no strength?

But thou, O LORD, art a shield for me; my glory, and the lifter up of mine head Psalms 3:3

The hardest journey of my life continues...

> *Prayer For Today: Lord I know that even at my weakest point, on the verge of giving up, you are the lifter of my head. Amen.*

Disbelief: inability or refusal to accept that something is true or real.

Every day since September 14, 2017, disbelief is a word I've used more times than I can count. Disbelief, surreal, unbelievable, shocked, and surprised are words that flood my brain and crowd my heart. I can't bring myself to believe my father is no longer with us. I beg someone to wake me from this terrible nightmare, so I can embrace my dad one more time, hear his voice one more time, or just tell him I love him one more time.

Echoing over the loud thoughts in my head and the pounding of my heart repeatedly breaking in a million pieces, I hear a calm familiar reminder: lean not unto my own understanding. As I said before, this has become my saving grace. It has spoken to my storm. I must continue to remind myself that I don't have the ability to understand this on my own. *My* ability can't feel beyond the pain. *My* ability can't see beyond this tragic event. *My* ability can't imagine being without my dad. I find comfort in knowing the omniscient, all-wise God knew this day would come. It also helps me to know the very thing that Dad instilled in me, the word of God and love for God, would be exactly what I need to get through the toughest days of my life. Even amid the raging storm of grief, I can still hear a still small voice that encourages me to lean on God. When I lean on God, he shows me with him, I have that ability to feel through the pain. With God, I have that ability to see beyond this tragic event. With God, I have that ability to realize I'm never without Daddy. Not only is he in my heart, but I can see him in my laugh, smile, mannerisms, and ministry. Despite being in utter disbelief, I can still whisper this prayer "Lord, help my unbelief". As I lie down, I realize God allowed me one more day to be everything my dad instilled in me.

My transparent moment: I can't believe this nightmare. I have got to wake up!

I had fainted, unless I had believed to see the goodness of the Lord in the land of the living. Wait on the Lord: be of good courage, and he shall strengthen thine heart: wait I say, on the Lord. Psalms 27:13-14

The journey continues...

> *Prayer For Today: Lord although I'm having a hard time accepting this reality, please strengthen my heart and increase my faith and trust in you. Amen.*

Angry: filled with anger: having a strong feeling of being upset or annoyed. : showing anger.

I am so angry!! The intensity of my emotions today has me furious, mad, upset, irritated, agitated, frustrated, and enraged. I'm all the above at the same time! Why did Daddy have to leave me? Why did God call him home now? Why didn't I have more time? Why does it hurt so bad? It just doesn't seem fair. I'm angry because people expect that I should be farther along in this process. I'm sorry, I didn't know there was a rule book on how long I'm allowed to grieve. I've only had my Dad my entire life, so excuse me if I have no idea how to do life without him. I've had to tell myself not only one day at a time, but one moment at a time.

I've decided to allow myself to feel how I feel until I feel different. No more suppressing emotions and trying to pretend I'm okay. I am not okay! Yes, I'm a Christian, and yes, I'm an evangelist, but right now I'm angry! I don't want to physically hurt anyone; I don't want to hurt myself, but I do wish that Christians would stop acting like it's not okay to be human.

Instead of pushing people, we need to let people be where they are in the process and pray that God will comfort and strengthen them during the most painful event of their lives. I miss Daddy so terribly that at times it's hard to breathe. When I can't find the words to pray, I hear the melody "He intercedes for me", by Kirk Franklin. As tears roll down my face, I long for better days.

My transparent moment: I can't breathe. I want to scream every time someone says, "You have to stop crying and be strong". I don't *have* to do anything!

Be ye angry, and sin not: let not the sun go down upon your wrath. Ephesians 4:26

The journey continues…

Prayer For Today: Lord please don't let my anger cause me to do or say something that is not pleasing to you. Help me to process the feelings and give me a peace knowing that you are in control of my life and you didn't bring me this far to leave me. Amen.

Lost: unable to find your way

I am so lost. I can't seem to find my way through this grieving process. It's a maze of ups and downs, twists and turns, that leads me back to heartache and despair. I feel like I'm wandering around life. I don't know which way to go, or what to do next. My thoughts overtake me, and I feel trapped in an emotional hole I can't escape. And no one seems to recognize just how lost and hurt I am. I often wonder if anyone can truly see my pain, and if they did, *would* they help me, or *could* they help me?

I'm so lost without Daddy. He was my God-given tour guide through this thing called life. He was there from day one helping me find my way and teaching me the ways of God. He spent my lifetime preparing me for this day. He knew it would come. Daddy taught me so much. I wonder if I took full advantage of every life lesson? Did I absorb all the knowledge he imparted to me? I know he left me well prepared, yet I'm still so lost. I can't even dig deep within and find the tools he left me. Where do I start? What now? How will I make it? Will I ever find my way? Guide me oh thou Great Jehovah. Lord don't let me wander in this wilderness too long.

My transparent moment: Is there anyone who can help me find my way? Is anyone even capable of helping me? I don't know.

I will instruct thee and teach thee in the way which thou shalt go: I will guide thee with mine eye. Psalms 32:8

The journey continues...

Prayer For Today: Lord even when I feel lost and confused, help me to remember you are the way and you will give me clarity and understanding. Amen.

Empty: containing nothing; not filled or occupied, desolate, deserted, abandoned

I sit here staring out the window feeling abandoned. Daddy didn't have permission to leave me; I wasn't ready. Who am I kidding? I would have never been ready for that day. Now it's here, and I have no tears and no words. I am empty. This hollow feeling is like nothing I've ever experienced. It's one thing to *say* you have nothing to give, but it's another thing when you unequivocally have nothing! Make no mistake about it, I'm burnt out. Like a well that has run dry, I have nothing more to offer. I've given encouragement, a shoulder to cry on, a listening ear, and pretty much everything any of my loved ones needed during this difficult time. We've all suffered such a great loss and I've stepped in when I could to help ease the pain. Now I sit here feeling completely depleted. I have nothing more to give. I can't even articulate this! I lift my head to God, but I don't have words. I only have tears & pain.

My transparent moment: I don't have anything left to give. I don't have anything left.

Now the God of hope fill you with all joy and peace in believing, that ye may abound in hope, through the power of the Holy Ghost. Romans 15:13

The journey continues...

Prayer For Today: Lord hear my heart's cry. Amen.

Sensitive: highly responsive or susceptible: such as easily hurt or damaged; *especially*: **easily hurt emotionally.**

I used to be a sensitive child who would cry at the drop of a dime. I would run to my daddy whenever someone hurt my feelings. Daddy had a way of making everything better. As part of growing up, I became less sensitive, but I still had Daddy to rescue me. During this grieving process, I've come to realize that I've become extra sensitive. I find myself breaking down suddenly. I could be watching a movie, listening to a song, sitting at work, or even speaking at church, and boom! It hits me afresh that my daddy is gone! As the tears flow, I try to focus on the good times and everything he taught me, but it's hard to accept the reality that he is no longer here. I beg God to wake me up from this nightmare but eventually resolve in my mind that there is no changing what has happened. As much as we dread it, avoid it, or don't want to talk about it, death is a part of life! I'm emotionally unstable, I don't know what to expect next. This dreadful journey continues...

My transparent moment: I cry so easily now. This nightmare makes me cry; I pout when I don't wake up from it. Lord, I know I will see him again, but I want him here now!

Set your affection on things above, not on things on the earth Colossians 3:2

The journey continues...

Prayer For Today: Lord, although I'm sensitive and extremely emotional, help me to realize that this is part of the process and you are here to comfort me. Amen.

Afraid: filled with fear or <u>apprehension</u>.

I opened my eyes this morning to a brand-new day. A day I'm grateful for, yet a day without my daddy. I'm so afraid of living life without him. Until September 14, 2017, I've never had to live a day without him. What will I do when I need to talk to him? How will I cope when I'm in trouble? Who will I depend on? Daddy was always there for me when I needed him. It's a scary feeling knowing my encourager, my protector, my rock is no longer a phone call away. The future seems so uncertain, but since Daddy taught, shared, and lived the word of God, I know my future *is* certain. I will see him again. It still hurts, and I'm still afraid so I enlist the help of Almighty God to help me find my way.

My transparent moment: I'm in a low place. Having to live without Daddy frightens me to my very core!

Fear thou not; for I am with thee: be not dismayed; for I am thy God: I will strengthen thee; yea, I will help thee; yea, I will uphold thee with the right hand of my righteousness. Isaiah 41:10

The journey continues...

Prayer For Today: Lord, I'm tired, weak, and afraid that I'm not going to make it through this journey. With each new day, the pain worsens. Please strengthen me for this journey. Amen.

Misunderstood: fail to interpret or understand the words or actions of (someone) correctly.

I've discovered while going through this grieving process, I've often been misunderstood by others. People have questioned my faith and my walk with God because I'm not grieving how a Christian *should* grieve. What does that even mean? I have come to realize everyone grieves differently. There is no right or wrong way to grieve. As I've known all along, there is no rule book or time limit for grief. We are human, and we feel, even as Jesus himself felt agony and pain. My faith in God should not be questioned, nor should my Christianity be attacked based on how I grieve.

I believe the most dangerous thing you can do is suppress feelings and hold emotions in just to keep up appearances. I refuse to hide behind a mask to appear to be okay on the outside while I sink into a deep hole of despair on the inside. One thing I can truly say is that my dad's death has allowed me to face and embrace every emotion despite how painful some of them may be. I've become free of people's opinions. Grief is liberating. I trust and love God and sometimes I hurt. Sometimes I don't quite understand, and that is perfectly okay. As I continue through this journey, I pray to God that people are more compassionate and understanding.

My transparent moment: People don't understand me. They don't understand my pain.

Judge not, that ye be not judged. For with what judgment ye judge, ye shall be judged: and with what measure ye mete, it shall be measured to you again. Matthew 7:1-2

The journey continues...

Prayer For Today: Lord, help us not to cast judgment or make assumptions about others based on the limited information we have. Help us to realize that everyone is struggling with some kind of battle and we all need your grace and mercy. Amen.

Sad: affected with or expressive of grief or unhappiness

Until Daddy left me, I never knew how it felt to be terribly sad for days, weeks, and now months. It just hurts so much. There is a deep sadness that plunges to the depths of my soul and it seems unreachable. Despite the warm hugs, kind gestures, and encouraging words, I'm still so deeply saddened. I long for the day the sadness eases up because honestly, it's exhausting carrying this burden. Some days the sadness is so unbearable that I beg my heart to stop feeling. For temporary relief sometimes, I zone out for several minutes, only to return to the worst pain I've ever felt. I feel like there is literally a hole in my heart.

My transparent moment: I've never been this sad. Why does it hurt so bad? Some days I'm not so sure I'll make it.

Cast thy burden upon the Lord, and he shall sustain thee: he shall never suffer the righteous to be moved. Psalms 55:22

And so, the journey continues…

> *Prayer For Today: Lord, please reach into the depths of my heart and soul and heal this pain only you can heal. Lord, please help me maintain. Amen.*

Distress: pain or suffering affecting the body, a body part, or the mind

I am conscious that this grief is affecting my mind, body, and soul. It's physically exhausting. I have no energy and some days no desire to even get out of the bed. I hurt everywhere. It's been a constant battle. My mind is always racing, and I can't find any relief. For the first 6 months after Dad's death, I dreamed of him every night. The same theme in every dream: Daddy came back to me. I was so excited, but each time I'd wake up and realize it was only a dream. My reality is Dad is gone, my heart is broken, my world is shattered, and my faith is shaken. This is my distress. I feel so disconnected and still can't find the words to pray. Would God even hear me if I could? I do have a solid foundation; Daddy made sure of that. I know it's only God who can pull me up out of this pit. I don't have a deep profound prayer, but I cry out to God! Lord, I need your help! I so desperately want God to rescue me from this dark place.

Transparent moment: This suffering is affecting every part of me. My heart can only feel pain. My body is worn out. My mind can't think.

In my distress I called upon the Lord and cried to my God: and he did hear my voice out of his temple, and my cry did enter into his ears. 2 Samuel 22:7

The journey continues...

Prayer For Today: Lord I need your help. Amen.

Emotional: subject to or easily affected by emotion

I've never been this in tune with my feelings. Grief has a way of opening every emotional pore. I've been on a roller coaster shifting from sad to shock, angry to alone, and heartbroken to empty, with no time to prepare for the next flood of emotions. During these eight months following Dad's death, I have had more emotional breakdowns than I care to count. A memory, a picture, a song, anything, or absolutely nothing, and I find myself an emotional wreck. With every tear that falls from my eyes, I feel like someone has punched me in the chest and my breathing has become shallow. Reality hit like a ton of bricks: Daddy is gone!! I find a secluded place as my emotions overtake me. I hear the phrase "Keep your head up", repeated in my head. I try to ignore it because the truth is, I don't have the strength to keep my head up. I'm not sure I even want to hold my head up. These emotions have me pinned in a corner & they are winning. I try to recall a scripture. I try to pray a detailed prayer, but today all I can muster up is a loud cry," Lord, you know. Psalms 46:1 is one of my favorite scriptures, but right now I can't recall the words. I do know I can ask for God's help anytime!

My transparent moment: This pain is a battle I never wanted, and it's winning.

God is our refuge and strength, a very present help in trouble. Psalms 46:1

The journey continues...

Prayer For Today: Lord, when I can't find the words to pray, please intercede on my behalf. Amen.

Blessed: bringing happiness or comfort:

As I sit here thinking of Daddy, I realize how blessed I am. I'm blessed because God gave me a daddy who was present and available. I'm blessed because my daddy was in my life, my entire life. Not everyone knows what it is to grow up with a father in the household. I don't take that for granted. I'm blessed because I never had to wonder if Daddy loved or cared for me. I didn't have to dream about what it would be like to have a father. I experienced it first- hand. Daddy spent countless hours with me, rearing me, taking care of me, providing for me, teaching me how to grill, teaching me the word of God, and supporting me 100%. I'm blessed because Daddy was able to see the fruit of his labor. He ate countless meals prepared by me, he saw me grow into a God-fearing woman, and he witnessed me teaching and preaching the word of God.

What a blessing to say my daddy taught me the things of God, created a platform for me, and allowed me to go forth under the anointing of the Holy Ghost on that same platform. I'm blessed because I could depend on my dad, and he always kept his word. I was able to step into a leadership role in the church and become the person that Daddy could depend on and look to for guidance. I'm grateful because I saw the proud look in his eyes as he bragged on his baby girl frequently. I'm abundantly blessed to have had him as my Daddy, my hero! Thank you, God, for your many blessings.

My transparent moment: I'm hurting, and I miss Daddy, but I am blessed.

The Lord bless thee, and keep thee: The Lord make his face shine upon thee, and be gracious unto thee: the Lord lift up his countenance upon thee and give thee peace. Numbers 6:24-26

The journey continues...

> *Prayer For Today: Lord, even in my darkest moments,*
> *help me to count my blessings and be grateful that you*
> *loved me so much that you gave me the best dad in the*
> *world. Amen.*

Peace: a state of tranquility or quiet

During this emotional roller coaster and mental chaos, over this past month, I've decided to allow myself some quiet alone time. In these moments I reflect on so many great memories with my Dad. I will forever cherish those moments, and they will never die. I think about Daddy having to deal with pain and physical limitations for several years, and how he never complained. He displayed great strength while suffering great hardship. I feel an immense peace knowing he will not have to suffer anymore. He made it through it, and he made it over. Eternal rest for him gives me peace that goes beyond my limited understanding. Sometimes we selfishly want to hold on to our loved ones, but we must realize when their time of suffering is over, they are ready to fly with the angels. It's comforting to know that even amid great pain and sorrow, God loves me enough to give me peace.

My transparent moment: Daddy suffered a long time. I have to let him fly.

Now the God of hope fill you with all joy and peace in believing, that ye may abound in hope, through the power of the Holy Ghost. Romans 15:13

The journey continues...

Prayer For Today: Thank you, Lord, for the moments of peace and tranquility that let me know Daddy is alright now. My loss is heaven's gain, and one day we'll meet again on the other side. Amen.

Joy: to experience great pleasure or delight: <u>rejoice</u>

Let me be honest. I don't take great pleasure or rejoice in the fact that Daddy is no longer here with me. If I had it my way, my daddy would still be here. However, I can rejoice in the fact that my Daddy has gone home to be with the Lord. It's a delight to know Daddy was saved, and he lived the life he preached. He always reminded me, "to be absent from the body, is to be present with the Lord". That is a reason to rejoice and thank God. Daddy is no longer in "the world of the dying" as he referred to it. He is now in the "land of the living" where there is no more death, no more sorrow, no more tears, and no more pain. Daddy is with the Savior! The physical pain he lived with daily is over. That most certainly is a reason to rejoice! As I continue to struggle with this journey that is far from a joyous one, I thank God for the moments of joy he allows me to have. At this point in my journey, I shed more tears than I rejoice, but I pray God can restore unto me joy overflowing!

My transparent moment: I rejoice in Daddy's blessing, but not in his departure.

Precious in the sight of the LORD is the death of his saints. Psalms 116:15

The journey, while often difficult, continues...

Prayer For Today: Lord, you are my joy. I need more of you! Amen.

Thankful: grateful, appreciative, filled with gratitude.

As I consider my life, I cannot help but thank God for giving me such an amazing father! I'm thankful that God gave me a father who loved and cared for his daughters. He took the time to show us how a man should treat a woman. Daddy set the bar by teaching us we deserved respect and nothing less. I'm grateful to God for all the great memories I have of my father. Daddy poured the word of God into me and taught me to depend on God under all circumstances. Daddy taught me how to effectively deliver a message, but that's not all. Daddy taught me to how to make the best barbecue ribs and chicken on this side of heaven!

I appreciate the time that Daddy spent with his family. Going to the drive-in movies was one of the things I really enjoyed growing up. I have so many precious memories, and I will cherish them always. I'm proud to continue my daddy's legacy. He didn't leave without passing his wisdom on to his children. Every time I mount the podium to deliver the word of God, I carry out his legacy. Every time I fire up the grill, his legacy continues. When I help someone, I am extending my daddy's legacy to them. Even when I crack a joke, his legacy lives on.

Daddy was one of the most selfless people in the world. He served and loved everyone he met. I shall never forget him, and I hope to always make him proud.

My transparent moment: I miss Daddy so much. This pain is more than I can understand, but I give God thanks for blessing me with the world's greatest daddy!

In every thing give thanks: for this is the will of God in Christ Jesus concerning you. I Thessalonians 5:18

The journey continues

Prayer For Today: Lord, thank you, for my daddy, Dr. H.A. Alexander, Sr. There will never be another one like him. I am grateful that I cannot be robbed of my

DNA, my memories, or the love Daddy showed me daily. Amen.

Love: strong affection for another arising out of kinship or personal ties

I've realized that the pain of losing my dad is so intense because I loved my daddy so much. I was Daddy's girl growing up. He spoiled me rotten. I can remember following my daddy everywhere, including the pulpit. Daddy would be up preaching, and I would be hugging his leg, holding on for dear life. He was my hero, my teacher, my provider, my everything. There wasn't a day that went by when I didn't know I was loved by my daddy. He was very protective of my mom and us three girls. He taught us what it was to be loved by someone with pure motives. He made sure his girls didn't have to depend on a man who was trying to manipulate and take advantage of them. We wanted for nothing. Dad made sure we didn't have to turn to others to fill any voids or "daddy issues". He taught us that men respect women, and we always deserved the ultimate respect. I'll cherish the last words he spoke to me "I love you sweetheart" for the rest of my days. I'm so glad that I could tell him I loved him as well. I don't have to wonder if Daddy loved me, or if he knew how much I loved him. Daddy not only told me daily, but he also showed me daily. Love is a beautiful thing, and I'm so glad that God gave me a loving father. Many go through life never experiencing the true love of a father, so even in my pain, I am blessed with his love forever in my heart.

My transparent moment: I'm hurting, but I have countless memories of true love to comfort me.

Love is patient, love is kind. It does not envy, it does not boast, it is not proud.

It does not dishonor others, it is not self-seeking, it is not easily angered, it keeps no record of wrongs. Love does not delight in evil but rejoices with the truth. It always protects, always trusts, always hopes, always perseveres. Love never fails. But where there are prophecies, they will cease; where there are tongues, they will be stilled; where there is knowledge, it will pass away.

1 Corinthians 13:4-8 NIV

The journey continues...

> *Prayer For Today: Lord I thank you for giving me a daddy that loved me with every fiber of his being. It hurts not having him here, but the love will forever be felt in my heart. Amen.*

Admiration: respect, appreciation, (high) regard, esteem.

As I sit and think about the great impact my daddy's death had me on me, I cannot help but think about the impact of his life! I have so much admiration and respect for my Daddy. He treated everyone kind whether other's thought they were deserving of it. He didn't discriminate against anyone. Even if there was a chance that he was being used, Daddy helped them anyway. He would say their motives were between them and God, and if they weren't pure, God would handle it. Amazingly, Daddy loved all people, even the ones who didn't love him. I admire how loving and caring Daddy treated others. He often told me, "We're not responsible for others' actions, but we are responsible for our reactions". What a powerful lesson! At times I struggled with this and my reactions were often abrasive. In true form, Dad loved me through my hard-headed moments. Dad always saw greatness in me and admonished me to love beyond my feelings.

Though Dad was stern, he was patient. He taught me that loving people as God loves is what is required of me.

What a great man of God I had! I'm so proud to call him Daddy! I salute my dad for living a life that was not only pleasing to God but a great example to his family. Well done Servant. Rest on. I will see you on that great getting up morning.

My transparent moment: This pain does not compare to the love of Daddy.

For the Lord himself shall descend from heaven with a shout with the voice of the archangel, and with the trump of God: and the dead in Christ shall rise first; then we which are alive and remain shall be caught up together with them in the clouds, to meet the Lord in the air; and so shall we ever be with the Lord. Wherefore comfort one another with these words. 1 Thess 4:16-18

The journey continues...

Prayer For Today: Lord I thank you for blessing me with an amazing dad who taught and showed me love. Amen.

Conclusion

As painful as it may be, this journey has taught me how to be present for my feelings and allow myself to process those feelings. Instead of holding in my emotions, I am experiencing freedom by releasing them. I realize now that internalized pain can literally kill. I hope I have provided insight into the highs and lows of grief. I've concluded that this process is never-ending. As long as we live, we will miss our loved ones. We are human, it will hurt not having them here physically with us, but through hope and healing, the memories of our loved one can bring great comfort and strength.

While grief is real and extremely painful, everyone goes through their process in their own way and at their own speed. Although the feelings of loss are similar, we process those feelings differently, based on our experiences and connections we had with the loved ones we've lost. Often, we want to push people through the process, so they can be okay or "over it" because it makes us uncomfortable. It's not fair for us to force people into a place they have not yet arrived, and possibly never will. With compassion, we must meet people where they are in the process. Executing patience and love with others is always the solution. A calm environment is better than one that stirs up rage and resentment. I'm not an expert on grief, nor do I have all the answers. Sixteen months after Daddy's death I'm still experiencing extreme lows and emotional breakdowns. I still long for my daddy. I believe for me that the intensity of this pain I am feeling must be equivalent to the intensity of the love Daddy gave me. Despite my tears, that makes me smile!

I will never be okay with not having my Daddy physically here with me, but I'm grateful that God thought enough of me to give me the best guardian angel. I'll hold on tight to every memory we shared, knowing no one can ever take them away. I never thought I'd make it without Daddy, but here I am by the grace of God. It has not been easy, nor has it felt good, but I know my Dad is proudly watching over me. Every step I make, every achievement, every decision, I feel Dad watching and smiling. I've made some major adjustments and changes in my life.

I've stepped out of my comfort zone and started modeling. As scary as that was for me, I realize modeling is my passion and it has been a positive outlet for me. It took the most painful experience of my life to push me into one of the best decisions of my life. Daddy always knew I'd be great and that I would travel the world. I'm excited to see what the future holds. Whether it be ministry, modeling, or a combination, I'm ready. and when I go Daddy will be right there with me. As I mount the podium to speak, or rip a runway in a show, I can see my Daddy sitting in the front row smiling and rooting me on. I am and will forever be his "baby girl". I'll continue to cry when it hurts, laugh when I remember his sense of humor, smile when I can feel him near, and pray that God continues to give me strength for the journey.

Transparent moment: The journey continues...

Prayer: Lord continue to be with me as I go through this journey and deal with the new normal of not having my Daddy here with me. Thank you for giving to me a man second to none. He left a lasting impression of love

on my life and in my heart. I am forever grateful. Amen.

CPSIA information can be obtained
at www.ICGtesting.com
Printed in the USA
FFHW021110270519
52658470-58171FF